Toasty hand warmers

LEISURE ARTS, INC., Maumelle, Arkansas

Introduction

I've been obsessed with hand warmers for some time now. They are functional, fashionable and fast to make. A crocheter can use any stitch pattern to make a square or rectangle and seam the sides leaving a thumb opening to make a cute pair of mitts. This makes them a perfect My First project!

Let's continue your journey into this wonderful world of crochet and learn some new stitches, play with some simple shaping and have fun with the projects we make.

MEET MARLY BIRD

I honestly believe anybody can crochet, it just takes a little patience and guidance to get there. I've been crocheting for over 20 years and teaching others how to crochet for 19 of those years. I love to teach others and watch the "a-ha!" moment in their eyes when they get it.

I want to present a series of books that hold your hand through the process of crocheting various items. Things that you have been interested in making, have always wanted to make, or don't know you MUST make RIGHT NOW!

Books that will walk you through step-by-step how to make anything from hand mitts to sweaters.

Books that offer more than just instructions but offer tips, tricks, suggestions on how to make it your own.

Books that you will pass down to your kids to show them how you learned to crochet.

"If there is one place in life you can be bold it is in your crochet!"

Marly Bird™

Contents

What is so great about this book? It's full of basic skill level hand warmers.

Need help? Turn to Getting Started page 4, it will help you jump right in and tackle your first pair. Of course, I've given you my favorite hints and tips! Now, have fun creating your first hand warmers!

Basic Wristers 18

Basic Mittens 20

Hygge Muff 24

Runner's Mitts 28

Scrappy Warmers 32

Rainbow Mittens 36

Striped Warmers 40

Thistle Mitts 44

Wavy Mitts 48

Granny Warmers 52

Are you looking for information about hooks or trying to understand the symbols? Check out the General Instructions beginning on page 56. But if you need a stitch refresher you will find those in the Basic Crochet Stitches on pages 60 and 61.

Getting Started

Choosing yarn for your projects is an exciting part of the crochet process. The possibilities are endless! Here are some of the top things you should consider when picking out the yarn you want to use.

WEIGHT

When following a pattern you often want to have a finished item that is similar to the sample. However, we know that there are times when you want to use a different yarn. Yes, you can do that. But, when you choose the new yarn, it is important that you pay attention to the weight of the yarn used in the sample versus the weight of your new yarn choice.

The Craft Yarn Council (CYC) has made it easy for us crocheters to know the weights of yarn by assigning labels to them. We now have a standard to go by. On each of the patterns in this book, in the shopping list, you will find a symbol next to the yarn. That symbol indicates the CYC standard weight of the yarn used in the pattern. As long as you choose a yarn that has that same symbol or is that same weight, you should be good to go.

FIBER

Just as the weight of the yarn is important, so too is the fiber content. Not all fibers are the same. Each type of fiber has unique characteristics that must be taken into account when considering substitution (which is pretty much a pattern-by-pattern process).

Before you start a project, practice making the chain stitch. Make sure the chains are not too tight and are consistent in size. In order to keep the tension of the stitches as I make the foundation chain, I position my thumb and middle finger on the chain close to the hook after I make a couple. It helps prevent my chain from twisting and I can keep the perfect size.

Here are some examples:

Machine Washability

Mercerized merino, cotton and most acrylics are machine washable, but silk or pure wool are not.

Elasticity

This is the fiber's ability to stretch and contract, which affects an item's ability to regain its original shape. Animal fibers and some synthetics are stretchy, while plant fibers are not.

In general, the closer you stick to the recommended fiber type, the more predictable the results will be.

Word of caution—when you change the weight of yarn for a project not only will the size of the project change (assuming you adjust the gauge to get what works best for the yarn you are using) but your yarn amounts will change. So, be sure you have enough of the yarn you want to use.

COLOR

Color can be very intimidating and sometimes challenging for a crafter. It is a difficult thing for me as well. Here is a little tip I have to help you put colors together. When I am working on a new pattern that has multiple colors, I always take a look at the different fabrics that are available. I look for color combinations that I like or that are on-trend. When I find one, I then find yarn with the same or similar colors and go from there. Not hard, right?

The best way to go about choosing a new color for any project is to pick a color you love, choose a striping yarn or variegated yarn with colors you love, or use the color wheel to help you choose complementary colors or different hues/shades of a color. Then of course, you can always use my fabric tip from before to help you choose.

I put together colors that speak to me for all the projects in this book. For the most part they are soft and soothing but you will find a couple brighter options like the Scrappy Warmers. Here is the deal, these colors work great for me but if a particular color doesn't speak to you and you wish to change it, PLEASE DO! You officially have my permission.

There are three types of colors—primary, secondary, and tertiary. Primary colors are red, blue, and yellow. Secondary colors are created by mixing two primary colors to create orange, green, and purple. Tertiary colors are created by mixing adjacent primary and secondary colors creating yellow-orange, yellow-green, blue-green, blue-purple, red-purple, and red-orange.

> "Warm colors are happy and energetic while cool colors are soothing and peaceful. If you choose two colors on the color wheel that are directly opposite each other, they are complementary colors; which means you would have warm and cool colors that work well together."

When buying yarn for a project, always check the dye lots to make sure you have the same numbers, and always buy enough to make the entire project. Nothing worse than running out of yarn when you are nearly done with a project! I will always buy at least one more skein than what I think I need just to make sure I have enough for the project and the gauge swatch.

Now that we have explored colors, you can use several colors that all have the same temperature. Warm colors are yellow, orange, and red while cool colors are green, blue, and purple.

You can select 3 colors that are next to each other on the color wheel (such as red, red-purple, and purple).

You can also create a palette with one family of hues: pastels, for example, or neutrals.

Another choice is to use a tonal mood and choose several shades of a single color like burgundy, red, and pink, for instance. Then add some black, white, or cream for more depth.

GAUGE

You can crochet for years without worrying about gauge, but as you expand your skills and really fine-tune your technique, you will want to follow patterns and recreate those items in both style and size. That is where the term gauge becomes very important.

Every crochet fabric is made up of stitches and rows. Gauge is the number of stitches and rows it takes to make one square inch or one full repeat of fabric. In any pattern you will find the gauge the designer used to make that item. And as long as you get the same number of stitches and the same number of rows to equal the same measurement as written in the pattern then you are sure to get the same size as the designer intended.

Gauge isn't always important, such as when you're making a scarf, an afghan, a bag, or anything else for which a precise size isn't essential. But when size does matter, the right or wrong gauge can make or break the finished piece.

Things that affect gauge include the yarn, the hook size and brand, and the stitch pattern you use to make your project. Yarns of different weights produce different gauges.

"I like making string into something beautiful, what is your superpower?"

A bulkier yarn produces a larger stitch, for example, while a finer yarn produces a smaller stitch. Hooks and stitch size—the same yarn crocheted on different size hooks will have different gauges; the same can be said of different brands of hooks. Because you make a stitch by wrapping yarn around the hook, the size of the hook determines the size of the stitch.

As for the brand, different brands of hooks are styled to have different points, throats and shafts, and as a result a crocheter will crochet differently with different hooks. Therefore, it is important that when your gauge swatch is complete and you get a yarn and hook combination that works for you, be sure to stick with that exact hook throughout the project.

Gauge Swatches

Just as it is important to use the same hook you plan on using for your project, it is important that you use the same yarn for your gauge swatch as for your project, not the same brand in a different color. Different dyes can affect how a specific yarn crochets up, and believe it or not, a yarn in one color can give you a different gauge from the same yarn in a different color.

Make your swatch as follows:

1. Chain the stitch multiple for the stitch pattern you are going to use. Guesstimate about how many multiples you need to yield a fabric that is at least 5" (12.75 cm) wide.
2. Work in the stitch pattern for the number of rows of the row pattern repeat, then enough more rows to yield 5" (12.75 cm) tall.
3. Finish off, cut the strand of yarn, leaving an 8" (20.5 cm) tail.
4. Block the swatch in the same manner you plan to use for your finished project.

Measure Swatch

To measure your swatch, smooth it out on a flat surface. Pin the edges down if they're curling in—be careful not to stretch your swatch—and follow these steps:

1. Lay a ruler along a row of stitches and mark the beginning and end of 4" (10 cm) with straight pins.
2. Note the number of stitches or stitch pattern repeats in 4" (10 cm), fractions and all.
3. Lay your ruler along a vertical line of stitches, aligning the bottom of the ruler with the bottom of a stitch, and put a straight pin in to show where the first stitch begins. Place another straight pin 4" (10 cm) up.
4. Count the rows between the pins, fractions and all, and note the number of rows.

You now know the number of stitches or stitch pattern repeats, as well as rows or row pattern repeats you get with that yarn and that hook over 4" (10 cm). Check to see if those measurements are the same as what the pattern indicates you need. If it is spot on, lucky you!

If it is off, here is what you do. If the stitches are too many, then your stitches are too small and you need to go up a hook size. If the stitches are too few, then your stitches are too big and you need to go down a hook size. Easy as that. But, work another swatch to be sure using the different size hook will work.

Oh my, the dreaded gauge swatch! When you decide to create a project that needs to fit, that's the time for finding out the importance of a gauge swatch. Gauge swatches will save you time, money and tears with a completed design that fits properly and that you will love.

Blocking

For any finished item that you plan on washing at some point, you will want to actually wash the swatch. Treat the swatch as you would the finished item. Use soap, put it in the washer (if it is machine washable) and let it dry. Doing so will help you see how the fabric will behave after washing. Does it hold together? Does it pill? Does it stretch? All of these things are important to know before you spend your time using that yarn to make a full size item.

Those are the benefits of washing your swatch, but what about the blocking part? First, did you know that the given gauge in a pattern is the blocked gauge (unless noted differently)? That means, it is entirely possible to have a pre-blocked gauge of 3 stitch pattern repeats = 4" (10 cm) but after blocking the measurement can increase to 2 stitch pattern repeats = 4" (10 cm). Over the course of a full project that is a HUGE difference. Therefore, it is imperative that you know what the blocked gauge is of your swatch.

Now, for the most part, wet blocking acrylic yarn doesn't really do anything to change it, but when you are using a wool, like Chic Sheep by Marly Bird™, blocking is very important. Specifically, I suggest wet blocking.

Here are some basic crochet supplies—yarn, crochet hooks, yarn needles, ruler, tape measure, and stitch markers.

Just as I mentioned before, you will want to wash your swatch. For wool, I suggest hand washing the finished swatch in your sink and use a wool wash. When you do this you are giving that yarn a spa treatment. The yarn has been handled, tugged, pulled, crocheted and just needs a chance to relax and let the fibers settle into place. Not only will the yarn show its true beauty when cleaned but it will block even more beautifully.

After the swatch has had good wash, follow these steps to block it out.

1. Get as much water out of your swatch as you can *without* stretching or wringing it out.

Note: When you lift the piece out of the sink, lift it out in both hands, making sure not to let any part of it stretch down.

2. Without stretching the piece, spread it out on the towel and fold the ends of the towel over it; then gently and loosely roll up the towel to absorb more water.
3. Gently lay your piece out on the blocking board.

BLOCKING TIP:
I like to use the cardboard cutting boards from the fabric section of the big box store. The grid lines on the board make it easy to measure out and block my swatch or my finished piece.

NOTE: Before you use it, be sure to use a damp paper towel and wipe it down to get rid of any extra ink!

4. Spread your piece out the measurements of the piece as a guide.
5. Using straight pins, pin and smooth all pieces.
6. Allow the piece to air dry. Keep the piece out of the sun as that may cause discoloration. If you're in a hurry, you can get your piece to dry in a matter of hours by placing a fan in front of it.

The last thing to do after the swatch has been blocked is to unpin it from the blocking board, let it rest for a couple of minutes then measure it for gauge.

Hints & Tips

I'm a brand spanking new crocheter, where do I start?

First, welcome to the best club ever! Being a crocheter is AWESOME! Now, the first project I would start with would be the Basic Wristers on page 18. They are simple, small and super useful! It is especially great for those of you who feel like instant gratification takes too long because it is a FAST project.

Have fun with the project and pick a yarn that excites you. I made this design with a basic solid color yarn but it would be equally as fun in a striped yarn.

Why is the yarn choice important?

You want to make sure you do not get bored as you're working on a project that is all one stitch. By choosing a yarn with fun colors or variegated colors, you will be excited to work with the yarn. Couple that with the joy of seeing how the colors all work together as it is crocheted makes for a very enjoyable experience even though you are only doing one stitch.

Plus, after you make a pair of wristers, you can share them with your friends at the next crochet group you attend at a coffee shop.

When I add a new ball of yarn to a color changing yarn do I start in the same color place?

When working with any yarn that has a color sequence you have to make that choice. You can certainly start at any location and let it be a design feature. Or you can start at the exact same point of color sequence on the new ball of yarn as where the old ball left off. It all depends on the look you are going for on your project.

For example, the Rainbow Mittens on page 36 uses a yarn that has long color changes. When I made these mittens I wanted them to match so I made sure to start both mittens at the same place in the color sequence. But I could have easily just started wherever in the color sequence and let the mittens be similar but not identical in color and they would still be awesome.

If I am just folding over and seaming a square of rectangle, it appears I can easily adjust the size of my mitt by adding or eliminating rows. Is that true?

I wanted to keep the majority of these hand warmers simple in construction so you could make adjustments like that. Therefore, the quick answer is YES, you can easily adjust the size of the ones that are basic squares or rectangles by adding/eliminating a row or two.

Specifically, the Basic Wristers, Wavy Mitts, Thistle Mitts, and the Runner's Mitts can all be adjusted. This type of mitt construction really is handy (giggle) when you need to fit larger or smaller hands.

Love the stitch pattern but not the variegated yarn?

Not a problem, get a completely different look by choosing a solid color yarn to make the project. Or maybe choose to make it in stripes instead of a solid. Something to remember is that stitch patterns show more with solid colors (even solid stripes) than they do in variegated yarns. Therefore, changing up the color yarn could really make the stitch pattern POP!

Don't get lost, Look At Your Work!

I know this sounds really obvious but many crocheters get into a rhythm of actually crocheting and they forget to look at their work. Pay attention to the stitches you are making and the pattern they create. Instead of following a pattern blindly, look at the actual fabric and understand what the stitches you are using are creating. Doing so will help you recognize any irregularities or mistakes early. If something looks wrong with the pattern, maybe you forgot an increase in the granny square or you don't have as many stitches at the end of the row as you should, you can fix the problem before it gets more compounded.

Biggest piece of advice for beginners, Count Your Stitches!

That is right, after each row be sure to count your stitches. One stitch more or one stitch less often means a mistake in the row you just worked. If you catch the off count early it is easy enough, albeit a little slow, to fix by frogging back that one row and redoing it. You will not have to count forever but until you are comfortable with the hook, the yarn and the pattern, it is good practice to count.

I like to use stitch markers. I will place them on the work every 20 stitches or between every stitch repeat. That makes it easier to count overall but more importantly, I know sooner rather than later if I have a mistake if the count is off between stitch markers. Therefore, I only have to frog to the previous stitch marker instead of the entire row.

What is frogging?

The act of ripping out your work is called frogging. As you "rip it, rip it, rip it" (say it fast) out you make the sound like a frog.

Do I have to use the same hook size as the pattern suggest?

The hook size you will use on your project depends on the gauge YOU get with the hook you choose and the yarn YOU use for your project. When a pattern lists a hook size for that pattern, it is a suggested hook size, a place for you to start but you will end up using whatever size YOU need to get the same gauge as listed in the pattern.

TIP:

It is important to note that when pairing up a crochet hook to a pattern or to a project already started, you should check the metric measurement of the actual hook you want to use. I've seen hooks labeled as F (3.5mm) and F (3.75mm); this might seem a trivial difference but when working on a project that requires strict gauge, it is important that you are always using the same size.

I hate weaving in ends... what can I do?

Well, know that you are not alone with that opinion. Not many crocheters I know enjoy weaving in ends. BUT, it is a necessary evil. I am not a fan of just crocheting over ends so please do not do that. Take the time to properly weave in your ends.

The best way to make sure they do not come out is to leave ends that are at least 4-6" (10-15 cm) long. Then use a tapestry needle to weave the end into the fabric on the wrong side in at least 3 different directions.

Oh No, there is a knot in my yarn!

Ya, it happens. You will be crocheting along when all of a sudden there is a knot in the yarn from the manufacturer. Don't panic, it is just a simple little knot. The first thing I want to tell you is this, are you listening? No, really, are you listening? Okay, here it is...DO NOT CROCHET OVER THE KNOT!

That's right, you want to go ahead and back up to the edge of the work (I like to change colors or add new yarn at the edge whenever possible), leave yourself at least 4-6" (10-15 cm) of length, cut that yarn with the knot, then again leaving a 4-6" (10-15 cm) tail of the yarn, rejoin the yarn as you would if you were changing colors and carry on.

This makes for more ends to weave in, yes. But is also means you will have a better finished piece that doesn't have knots in the middle of the fabric. Plus, you have no idea if those knots are secure and the last thing you want is to have the knot come undone as you are wearing your hand warmers, right?

I made changes but I can't remember what I did!

This happens to me all the time, I get excited about a project or pattern and just want to work on it. Like many of you, I lie to myself by saying that I will remember what I did, then days go by, I pick up my pattern and I have no idea what I am doing.

Learn from my mistakes. The best piece of advice I can offer is to take notes as you are working on a project. If a pen and paper is your jam, great! Be sure to have a notebook next to you as you work on your project and jot down notes (yarn are you using, the needle size and brand, your gauge, the title of the book and the page number of the pattern you are using, etc.).

If you are more tech savvy, then pop open an app that you can keep notes in and use that for your notes. I know that every phone, pad, tablet

"Just as the old adage, 'When life gives you lemons, make lemonade', I like to say, 'When life hands you a tangled ball of yarn, make a new pair of mitts!'"

or whatnot has their own so I am not going to recommend any here.

The bottom line is this, taking notes is very important when you are working on any pattern. It is a place that you can keep track of the details of your pattern or even keep a tally of the number of repeats or rows you have completed. But notes are especially important if you're making changes to a pattern.

My mitts are two different sizes, what did I do?

Have no fear, this is perfectly normal for new crocheters (and honestly some experienced ones too). When we first work up a pattern we are uncertain about it and tend to be a little more loose than normal. Then, after finishing one mitt we start the second with more confidence and knowledge about the pattern and tend to tighten up our stitches.

To make sure that your project is not too far off gauge, I like to keep my tape measure handy so I can measure my piece as I work along. It only takes a few seconds and it saves me hours of work if I have to frog my project and redo it.

Or, if you are more free spirited and just want to chance it, make both hand warmers and if one is larger than the other, make another set to match the first then you will just have two sets of hand warmers.

Projects

Basic Wristers

BASIC

These wristers are a step beyond a swatch. They are simply made and with the ease of a seam you have a cute pair of hand warmers that are great to throw on when you go outside.

Shopping List

Yarn (Medium Weight)

MEDIUM 4

[3.5 ounces, 186 yards (100 grams, 170 meters) per skein]:

☐ 1 skein

Crochet Hook

☐ Size G (4.5 mm) **or** size needed for gauge

Finished Size:
9" long x 8½" hand circumference (23 cm x 21.5 cm)

GAUGE INFORMATION

In pattern,
18 dc and 9 rows = 4" (10 cm)

Gauge Swatch: 4" (10 cm) square
Ch 20.
Work same as Body for 9 rows: 18 dc.
Finish off.

WRISTER (Make 2)

Body

Ch 43.

Row 1 (Wrong side)**:** Dc in third ch from hook **(2 skipped chs do not count as a st)** and in each ch across: 41 dc.

Note: Loop a short piece of yarn around the **back** of any stitch on Row 1 to mark **right** side.

Rows 2-19: Ch 2 **(does not count as a st)**, turn; dc in Back Loop Only of first dc and each dc across *(Fig. 2, page 59)*.

Joining Row: Ch 1, turn; fold piece in half with **wrong** side together, matching beginning ch to Row 19. Working through **both** loops on **both** pieces, slip st in first 28 dc; working in **both** loops of dc on front piece only, slip st in next 9 dc **(thumb opening)**, working through **both** loops on **both** pieces, slip st in last 4 dc; finish off.

Basic Mittens

BASIC

Use these mitts as you hit the slopes or if you just make snowballs. With the thick solid yarn, you will not have any worry of snow sinking into the mitten. With bulky yarn and a big crochet hook, you have a project that can be done in a couple hours!

Shopping List

Yarn (Super Bulky Weight)

SUPER BULKY 6

[10.5 ounces, 193 yards
(300 grams, 177 meters)
per skein]:

☐ 1 skein

Crochet Hook

☐ Size L (8 mm)
or size needed for gauge

Additional Supplies

☐ Yarn needle

Finished Size:
9½" long x 10" hand circumference
(24 cm x 25.5 cm)

GAUGE INFORMATION

8 hdc and 6 rows = 4" (10 cm)

Gauge Swatch: 1¾" (4.5 cm) diameter

Work same as Hand through Rnd 1: 8 hdc.

STITCH GUIDE

HALF DOUBLE CROCHET 2 TOGETHER ***(abbreviated hdc2tog)*** (uses next 2 sts)

(YO, insert hook in **next** hdc, YO and pull up a loop) twice, YO and draw through all 5 loops on hook **(counts as one hdc)**.

MITTEN (Make 2)

Hand

Rnd 1 (Right side)**:** Make an adjustable loop to form a ring ***(Figs. 1a-d, page 58)***; ch 1, work 8 hdc in ring; join with slip st to first hdc: 8 hdc.

Note: Loop a short piece of yarn around any stitch to mark Rnd 1 as **right** side.

Rnd 2: Ch 1, hdc in same st as joining, 2 hdc in next hdc, (hdc in next hdc, 2 hdc in next hdc) around; join with slip st to first hdc: 12 hdc.

Rnd 3: Ch 1, hdc in same st as joining and in next hdc, 2 hdc in next hdc, (hdc in next 2 hdc, 2 hdc in next hdc) around; join with slip st to first hdc: 16 hdc.

Rnd 4: Ch 1, hdc in same st as joining and in next 6 hdc, 2 hdc in next hdc, hdc in next 7 hdc, 2 hdc in next hdc; join with slip st to first hdc: 18 hdc.

Rnds 5-8: Ch 1, hdc in same st as joining and in each hdc around; join with slip st to first hdc.

Do **not** finish off.

Right Thumb Opening

Rnd 1: Ch 1, hdc in same st as joining and in next 3 hdc, ch 5 **(thumb opening)**, skip next 3 hdc, hdc in last 11 hdc; join with slip st to first hdc; do **not** finish off: 15 hdc and 5 chs.

Left Thumb Opening

Rnd 1: Ch 1, hdc in same st as joining and in next 10 hdc, ch 5 **(thumb opening)**, skip next 3 hdc, hdc in last 4 hdc; join with slip st to first hdc; do **not** finish off: 15 hdc and 5 chs.

Cuff

Rnds 1-4: Ch 1, hdc in same st as joining and in each st around; join with slip st to first hdc: 20 hdc.

Rnd 5: Ch 1, hdc in same as joining and in next 4 hdc, hdc2tog twice, hdc in last 11 hdc; join with slip st to first hdc: 18 hdc.

Thumb

Rnd 1: With **right** side facing, join yarn with slip st in same st as last hdc on Rnd 1 of Thumb opening; ch 1, hdc in same st as joining and in next 3 hdc, hdc in same st as first hdc on Rnd 1 of Thumb Opening; hdc in free loop of next 5 chs ***(Fig. 3, page 59)***; join with slip st to first hdc: 10 hdc.

Rnd 2: Ch 1, hdc in same st as joining and in each hdc around; join with slip st to first hdc.

Rnd 3: Ch 1, hdc in same st as joining, (hdc2tog, hdc in next hdc) around; join with slip st to first hdc: 7 hdc.

Rnd 4: Ch 1, sc in same st as joining and in each hdc around; join with slip st to first sc, finish off leaving a long end for sewing.

Thread yarn needle with long end and weave needle through sts on Rnd 4 ***(Fig. 5, page 59)***; pull tightly to close hole and secure end.

True Story

I have lived in Colorado most of my life and have never been skiing. Once, when I was a sophomore in University I did attempt to go snowboarding and never made it off the bunny slope. So, when I suggest that this set would be great to hit the slopes, I should also mention that it will look FANTASTIC in the lodge as you are crocheting the day away with a cup of Irish Coffee (ask me how I know *wink).

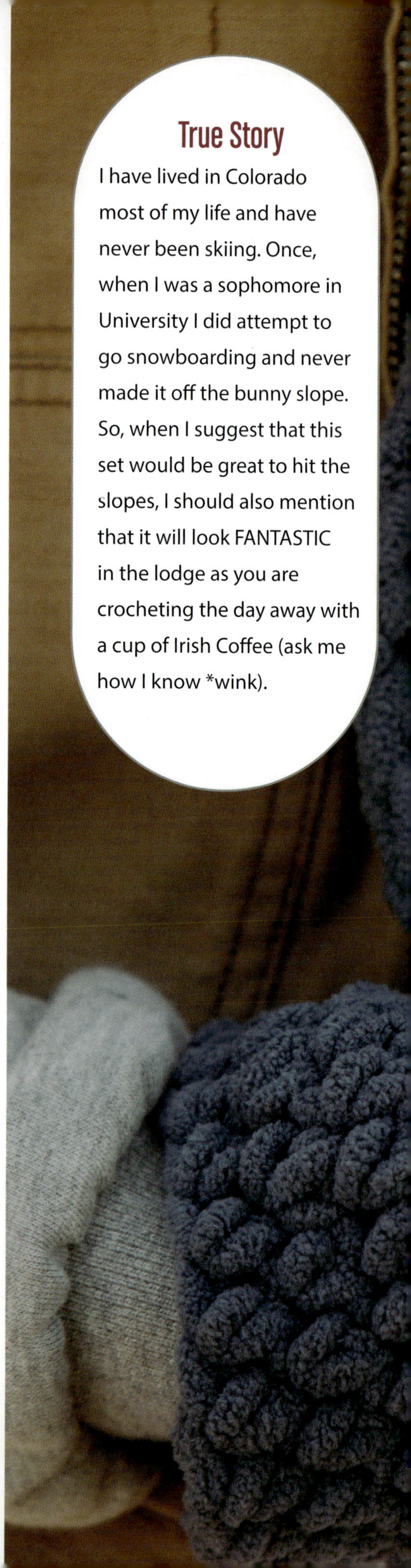

Hygge Muff

BASIC

This reversilbe muff with wrist strap is a must-have in my outdoor sporting event accessory bag (along with a blanket and stadium chair). I find I don't always want to put on a pair of mittens while I watch a game, so the muff is great. It is perfect for snuggling my hands into while sitting in the stands but I can pull them out quickly to clap for my boys on the field.

Shopping List

Yarn (Bulky Weight)

BULKY 5

[5 ounces, 132 yards
(141 grams, 121 meters)
per skein]:

☐ Grey - 2 skeins

(Super Bulky Weight)

SUPER BULKY 6

[10.5 ounces, 193 yards
(300 grams, 177 meters)
per skein]:

☐ Dark Grey - 1 skein

Crochet Hook

☐ Size N/P (10 mm)
or size needed for gauge

Finished Size:
12" wide x 10" high flattened
(30.5 cm x 25.5 cm)

GAUGE INFORMATION

With two strands of Grey,
7 hdc and 6 rows = 4" (10 cm)

Gauge Swatch: 4" (10 cm) square
With two strands of Grey, ch 9.
Work same as First Side for 6 rows:
7 hdc.
Finish off.

TWISTED CORD HANDLE

Cut 2 pieces of Grey, each 40" (101.5 cm) long. Holding both pieces together, fold in half; then twist until **tight**. Fold in half and let it twist itself, tie a knot to secure the loose ends.

FIRST SIDE

Holding two strands of Grey together, make a slip knot and place on hook, insert hook through both folded ends of the twisted cord, YO and pull through both loops on cord and slip knot on hook; ch 36.

Row 1 (Right side)**:** Hdc in third ch from hook and in each ch across: 34 hdc.

Note: Loop a short piece of yarn around any stitch to mark Row 1 as **right** side.

Row 2: Ch 2 **(does not count as a st, now and throughout)**, turn; hdc in first hdc and in each hdc across.

Repeat Row 2 until piece measures approximately 12" (30.5 cm) from beginning ch.

Finish off.

SECOND SIDE

With one strand of Dark Grey, ch 36.

Row 1 (Wrong side)**:** Hdc in third ch from hook and in each ch across: 34 hdc.

Note: Loop a short piece of yarn around the **back** of any stitch on Row 1 to mark **right** side.

Row 2: Ch 2, turn; hdc in first hdc and in each hdc across.

Repeat Row 2 until piece measures approximately 12" (30.5 cm) from beginning ch; do **not** finish off.

Joining: Ch 1, with **wrong** sides and beginning chs of both pieces together and working through **both** thicknesses, sc in each hdc across and in end of each row across; sc in free loop of each ch across ***(Fig. 3, page 59)*** and in end of each row across; join with slip st to first sc, do **not** finish off.

Side joining row: Fold piece in half matching short edges and having First Side outside, slip st in each sc across short edge, leave remaining sc unworked; finish off.

Change It Up!

It would be fun to make this muff a little bit longer so that two people could use it at the same time. To do that you double the number of rows for the length of the muff. Then, when you seam it up leave an opening for the hands to fit in as you sit side by side with somebody. This opening can be one large one around the center or two individual ones at about the 1/3 mark from either side opening.

Runner's Mitts

BASIC

These small mitts are great for the person on the run, literally or figuratively. The reflective yarn bounces light off the mitts making you more visible. They also have a simple pocket on the top of the hand that is just the right size for a credit card or key card or just a tissue.

Shopping List

Yarn (Bulky Weight)

BULKY 5

[3.5 ounces, 88 yards (100 grams, 80 meters) per skein]:

- ☐ Grey - 1 skein
- ☐ Purple - 1 skein

Crochet Hook

- ☐ Size I (5.5 mm) **or** size needed for gauge

Additional Supplies

- ☐ Yarn needle
- ☐ Sewing needle and matching thread
- ☐ ⅜" (10 mm) buttons - 2

Finished Size:

4¾" long x 8" hand circumference (12 cm x 20.5 cm)

GAUGE INFORMATION

12 sc and 15 rows = 4" (10 cm)

Gauge Swatch: 4" (10 cm) square

Ch 13.

Work same as Body for 14 rows: 12 sc.

Finish off.

MITT (Make 2)

With Grey, ch 25.

Row 1 (Right side)**:** Sc in second ch from hook and in each ch across: 24 sc.

Note: Loop a short piece of yarn around any stitch to mark Row 1 as **right** side.

Rows 2 and 3: Ch 1, turn; sc in each sc across.

Finish off.

Row 4: With **wrong** side facing, join Purple with sc in first sc ***(see Joining With Sc, page 58)***; sc in each sc across.

Rows 5-18: Ch 1, turn; sc in each sc across.

Joining Row: Ch 1, do **not** turn; fold piece in half with **wrong** side together, matching ends of rows. Working through **both** thicknesses, slip st in first 10 rows, working in ends of rows on front piece only, slip st in next 5 rows **(thumb opening)**, working through **both** thicknesses, slip st in last 3 rows; finish off.

POCKET **(Make 2)**

With Grey, ch 10.

Row 1 (Wrong side)**:** Sc in second ch from hook and in each ch across: 9 sc.

Note: Mark the **back** of any stitch on Row 1 to as **right** side.

Rows 2-10: Ch 1, turn; sc in each sc across.

Row 11: Ch 1, turn; sc in first 4 sc, (sc, ch 3, sc) in next sc **(button loop made)**, sc in last 4 sc; finish off leaving a long end for sewing.

Using photo as a guide for placement, place Pocket on back side of Mitt having thumb opening at side and matching bottom edges. Sew sides and bottom to Mitt leaving top open.

Sew button to Mitt opposite button loop.

True Story

I have a lot of runners in my neighborhood and they run at all hours of the day and night. Well, one night as I was driving home, it was super dark outside and I barely saw a woman running along the street. She had no reflective clothing on that I could see and I'm lucky that I didn't hit her! Anyway, it was after that I thought about the reflective yarn from Red Heart and decided that a simple pair of gloves the runner could wear might help with the visibility problem. Thus, these mitts were created.

Scrappy Warmers

BASIC

I **am so in love with these arm warmers! They are stylish, warm and have just the right amount of color.**

Finished Size:
17" (43 cm) long x
9" (23 cm) hand circumference x
11½" (29 cm) upper arm circumference

GAUGE INFORMATION

In Hand pattern,
18 hdc and 12 rows = 4" (10 cm)
Gauge Swatch: 4" (10 cm) square
Ch 20.
Work same as Hand for 12 rows: 18 hdc.
Finish off.

STITCH GUIDE

PUFF STITCH (uses one st)
YO, insert hook in st indicated, YO and pull up a loop even with loop on hook, (YO, insert hook in **same** st, YO and pull up a loop even with loop on hook) twice, YO and draw through all 7 loops on hook, ch 1 to close.

ARM WARMER (Make 2)

Hand

With Brown and leaving a long end for sewing, ch 38.

Row 1 (Wrong side)**:** Hdc in third ch from hook **(2 skipped chs do not count as a st)**, hdc in each ch across: 36 hdc.

Note: Loop a short piece of yarn around the **back** of any stitch on Row 1 to mark **right** side.

Rows 2-17: Ch 2, turn; hdc in Back Loop Only of first hdc and each hdc across ***(Fig. 2, page 59)***.

Row 18 (Joining row)**:** Ch 2, turn; hdc in Back Loop Only of first hdc and each hdc across; join with slip st to horizontal bar of first hdc ***(Fig. 4, page 59)***.

Body

Rnd 1: Do **not** turn; hdc in horizontal bar of same st as joining and each hdc around; do **not** join, place marker to indicate beginning of round ***(see Markers, page 58)***.

Rnd 2: Hdc in horizontal bar of each hdc around.

Rnd 3: Hdc in horizontal bar of each hdc around changing to Blue in last hdc made ***(Fig. 6, page 59)***; do **not** cut Brown.

Shopping List

Yarn (Medium Weight)

[3.5 ounces, 186 yards (100 grams, 170 meters) per skein]:
☐ Brown - 1 skein
☐ Blue - 1 skein
☐ Green - 1 skein
☐ Pink - 1 skein

Crochet Hook
☐ Size G (4 mm)
or size needed for gauge

Carry Brown loosely along **wrong** side of work throughout.

Rnd 4: Working in both loops, (work Puff St in next hdc, skip next hdc) around changing to Brown in last st made; cut Blue: 18 Puff Sts and 18 chs.

Rnd 5: Working in both loops, hdc in each Puff St and in each ch around: 36 hdc.

Rnd 6: ★ Hdc in horizontal bar of next 17 hdc, 2 hdc in horizontal bar of next hdc; repeat from ★ once **more**: 38 hdc.

Rnd 7: Hdc in horizontal bar of each hdc around.

Rnd 8: Hdc in horizontal bar of each hdc around changing to Green in last hdc made.

Rnd 9: Working in both loops, (work Puff St in next hdc, skip next hdc) around changing to Brown in last st made; cut Green: 19 Puff Sts and 19 chs.

Rnd 10: Working in both loops, hdc in each Puff St and in each ch around: 38 hdc.

Rnds 11 and 12: Hdc in horizontal bar of each hdc around.

Rnd 13: Hdc in horizontal bar of each hdc around changing to Pink in last hdc made.

Rnd 14: Working in both loops, (work Puff St in next hdc, skip next hdc) around changing to Brown in last st made; cut Pink: 19 Puff Sts and 19 chs.

Rnd 15: Working in both loops, hdc in each Puff St and in each ch around: 38 hdc.

Rnd 16: ★ Hdc in horizontal bar of next 18 hdc, 2 hdc in horizontal bar of next hdc; repeat from ★ once **more**: 40 hdc.

Rnd 17: Hdc in horizontal bar of each hdc around.

Rnd 18: Hdc in horizontal bar of each hdc around changing to Blue in last hdc made.

Rnd 19: Working in both loops, (work Puff St in next hdc, skip next hdc) around changing to Brown in last st made; cut Blue: 20 Puff Sts and 20 chs.

Rnd 20: Working in both loops, hdc in each Puff St and in each ch around: 40 hdc.

Rnds 21 and 22: Hdc in horizontal bar of each hdc around.

Rnd 23: Hdc in horizontal bar of each hdc around changing to Green in last hdc made.

Rnd 24: Working in both loops, ★ work Puff St in next hdc, skip next hdc; repeat from ★ around changing to Brown in last st made; cut Green: 20 Puff Sts and 20 chs.

Rnd 25: Working in both loops, hdc in each Puff St and in each ch around: 40 hdc.

Rnd 26: ★ Hdc in horizontal bar of next 9 hdc, 2 hdc in horizontal bar of next hdc; repeat from ★ around: 44 hdc.

Rnd 27: Hdc in horizontal bar of each hdc around.

Rnd 28: Hdc in horizontal bar of each hdc around changing to Pink in last hdc made.

Rnd 29: Working in both loops, ★ work Puff St in next hdc, skip next hdc; repeat from ★ around changing to Brown in last st made; cut Pink: 22 Puff Sts and 22 chs.

Rnd 30: Working in both loops, hdc in each Puff St and in each ch around: 44 hdc.

Rnds 31-33: Hdc in horizontal bar of each hdc around.

Finish off.

With **wrong** side of Hand together and matching ends of rows and using long beginning end, whipstitch seam for 2" (5 cm) ***(Fig. 7, page 59)***, leaving a 2" (5 cm) thumb opening, whipstitch remaining seam together.

Bright Idea!

Make a matching set. Use the pattern stitch from the arm of these scrappy stripes arm warmers to make a cowl.

Rainbow Mittens

BASIC

There is a hole in my mitten! Yep, it is supposed to be there. These mittens start out with a cuff, then the hand, the thumb and when we get to the fingers near the top of the mittens, we add a simple hole where the forefinger of each hand would be. Why add the hole? So you can sneak your finger out of the mitten to send a text, use your camera or scratch your nose without having to take off your entire mitten. It's a small hole and won't be noticeable with general wear but it is very useful.

Shopping List

Yarn (Medium Weight)

MEDIUM 4

[3.5 ounces, 187 yards (100 grams, 171 meters) per skein]:

☐ 1 skein

Crochet Hook

☐ Size J (6 mm)

or size needed for gauge

Additional Supplies

☐ Yarn needle

Finished Size:

10½" long x 9" hand circumference (26.5 cm x 23 cm)

GAUGE INFORMATION

In pattern,

10 hdc and 8 rows = 3" (7.5 cm)

Gauge Swatch:

4" wide (flattened) x 2¼" high (10 cm x 5.5 cm)

Work same as Cuff for 6 rnds: 36 sc.

STITCH GUIDE

HALF DOUBLE CROCHET 2 TOGETHER

(abbreviated hdc2tog)

(uses next 2 hdc)

Working in horizontal bars of each hdc ***(Fig. 4, page 59)***. (YO, insert hook in horizontal bar of **next** hdc, YO and pull up a loop) twice, YO and draw through all 5 loops on hook **(counts as one hdc)**.

MITTEN (Make 2)

Cuff

Ch 23; join with slip st to form a ring.

Rnd 1 (Right side)**:** Ch 1, sc in same ch and in each ch around; do **not** join, place marker to indicate beginning of round ***(see Markers, page 58)***: 23 sc.

Rnds 2-5: Sc in each sc around.

Rnd 6: Hdc in each sc around.

Working in horizontal bars of each hdc ***(Fig. 4, page 59)***.

Rnds 7-10: Hdc in each hdc around.

Gusset

Rnd 1: 2 Hdc in each of next 2 hdc, hdc in each hdc around: 25 hdc.

Rnd 2: 2 Hdc in next hdc, hdc in next 2 hdc, 2 hdc in next hdc, hdc in each hdc around: 27 hdc.

Rnd 3: 2 Hdc in next hdc, hdc in next 4 hdc, 2 hdc in next hdc, hdc in each hdc around: 29 hdc.

Rnd 4: 2 Hdc in next hdc, hdc in next 6 hdc, 2 hdc in next hdc, hdc in each hdc around: 31 hdc.

Rnd 5: 2 Hdc in next hdc, hdc in next 8 hdc, 2 hdc in of next hdc, hdc in each hdc around: 33 hdc.

Rnd 6: Hdc in next hdc, ch 3, skip next 10 hdc **(thumb opening)**, hdc in each hdc around: 23 hdc and 3 chs.

Rnd 7: Hdc in next hdc and in next 3 chs, hdc in each hdc around: 26 hdc.

Rnds 8-12: Hdc in each hdc around.

Right Hand

Rnd 1 (Finger Hole Rnd)**:** Hdc in next 9 hdc, ch 2, skip next 2 hdc, hdc in each hdc around: 24 hdc and 2 chs.

Rnd 2: (Hdc2tog, hdc in next hdc) 3 times, hdc in next 2 chs, (hdc2tog, hdc in next hdc) around: 18 hdc.

Rnd 3: Hdc2tog around: 9 hdc.

Rnd 4: Hdc in next hdc, hdc2tog around: 5 hdc.

Rnd 5: Hdc in next hdc, hdc2tog twice; slip st in next 2 hdc; finish off leaving a long end for sewing: 3 hdc.

Thread yarn needle with long end and weave needle through sts on Rnd 5 ***(Fig. 5, page 59)***; pull tightly to close hole and secure end.

Left Hand

Rnd 1 (Finger Hole Rnd)**:** Hdc in next 20 hdc, ch 2, skip next 2 hdc, hdc in each of next 4 hdc: 24 hdc and 2 chs.

Rnd 2: Hdc2tog, (hdc in next hdc, hdc2tog) 6 times, hdc in next 2 chs, hdc in next hdc, hdc2tog, hdc in next hdc: 18 hdc.

Beginning with Rnd 3, complete same as Right Hand.

Thumb - Both Sizes

Rnd 1: With **right** side facing, join yarn with hdc in first skipped hdc at thumb opening ***(see Joining With Hdc, page 58)***; hdc in next 9 hdc and in free loop of next 3 chs ***(Fig. 3, page 59)***; do **not** join; place marker to indicate beginning of round: 13 hdc.

Rnds 2-6: Hdc in each hdc around.

Rnd 7: Hdc in next hdc, hdc2tog around: 7 hdc.

Rnd 8: Hdc in next hdc, hdc2tog around: 4 hdc.

Rnd 9: Hdc2tog twice; finish off leaving a long end for sewing: 2 hdc.

Thread yarn needle with long end, sew hole closed.

Change It Up!

Instead of adding the hole, finish off the mitten as normal and you will have a basic pair of mittens. You can change it up even more by using one color of yarn vs multiple colors.

Striped Warmers

BASIC

Use any yarn you have laying around to get these cute striped arm warmers. A simple V-st is used to get a nice fabric and the stripes add something to a basic pattern.

Finished Size:
12" (30.5 cm) long
8" (20.5 cm) hand circumference
10½" (26.5 cm) upper arm circumference

GAUGE INFORMATION

In pattern,
5 V-Sts = 3½" (9 cm);
8 rows = 3¾" (9.5 cm)

Gauge Swatch: 3½" wide x 3¾" high (9 cm x 9.5 cm)

Ch 16.

Row 1: Work V-St in fifth ch from hook **(4 skipped chs count as one dc and one skipped ch)**, ★ skip next 2 chs, work V-St in next ch; repeat from ★ across to last 2 chs, skip next ch, dc in last ch: 4 V-Sts and 2 dc.

Rows 2-8: Ch 3 **(counts as first dc)**, turn; work V-St in each V-St (ch-1 sp) across, dc in last dc.

Finish off.

STITCH GUIDE

V-ST

(Dc, ch 1, dc) in st or sp indicated.

ARM WARMER (Make 2)

Hand Ribbing

With Ecru, ch 4.

Row 1: Sc in second ch from hook and in each ch across: 3 sc.

Row 2: Ch 1, turn; sc in Back Loop Only of each sc across *(Fig. 2, page 59)*.

Repeat Row 2 until Hand Ribbing measures approximately 8" (20.5 cm) slightly stretched.

Joining Row: Ch 1, turn; fold piece in half, working in free loops of beginning ch *(Fig. 3, page 59)* and in Back Loops Only of sc on last row, slip st in each st across; do **not** finish off.

Body

Foundation Rnd (Right side)**:** Ch 1, working in ends of rows across long edge of Hand Ribbing, work 26 sc evenly spaced around; join with slip st to first sc, finish off.

Note: Loop a short piece of yarn around any stitch to mark Foundation Rnd as **right** side.

Rnd 1: With **right** side facing, join Brown with dc in any sc *(see Joining With Dc, page 58)*; ch 1, dc in same st, skip next sc, (work V-St in next st, skip next sc) around; join with slip st to first dc, finish off: 13 V-sts.

Rnd 2: With **right** side facing, join Rust with dc in first V-St (ch-1 sp); ch 1, dc in same sp, work V-St in each V-St around; join with slip st to first dc, finish off.

Rnd 3: With **right** side facing, join Grey with dc in first V-St; ch 1, dc in same sp, work V-St in each V-St around; join with slip st to first dc, finish off.

Shopping List

Yarn (Medium Weight)

MEDIUM 4

[7 ounces, 370 yards (198 grams, 338 meters) per skein]:

- ☐ Ecru - 1 skein
- ☐ Brown - 1 skein
- ☐ Rust - 1 skein
- ☐ Grey - 1 skein

Crochet Hook

- ☐ Size H (5 mm) or size needed for gauge

Rnd 4 (Thumb Opening)**:** With **right** side facing, join Ecru with dc in first V-St; ch 1, dc in same sp, work V-St in each V-St around, ch 6; join with slip st to first dc, finish off: 13 V-sts and one ch-6 sp.

Rnd 5: With **right** side facing, join Brown with dc in first V-St; ch 1, dc in same sp, work V-St in each V-St around, work 2 V-Sts in next ch-6 sp; join with slip st to first dc, finish off: 15 V-Sts.

Rnd 6: With **right** side facing, join Rust with dc in first V-St; ch 1, dc in same sp, work V-St in each V-St around; join with slip st to first dc, finish off.

Rnd 7: With **right** side facing, join Grey with dc in first V-St; ch 1, dc in same sp, work V-St in each V-St around; join with slip st to first dc, finish off.

Rnd 8: With **right** side facing, join Ecru with dc in first V-St; ch 1, dc in same sp, work V-St in each V-St around; join with slip st to first dc, finish off.

Rnd 9: With **right** side facing, join Brown with dc in first V-St; ch 1, dc in same sp, work V-St in each V-St around; join with slip st to first dc, finish off.

Rnds 10-21: Repeat Rnds 6-9, 3 times.

Arm Ribbing

Foundation Rnd: With **right** side facing, join Rust with sc in first dc ***(see Joining With Sc, page 58)***; sc in each ch and in each dc around; join with slip st to first sc: 45 sc.

Row 1: Ch 4, sc in second ch from hook and in each ch across; slip st in same st as joining on Foundation Rnd and in next sc on Foundation Rnd: 3 sc.

Row 2: Ch 1, turn; skip first 2 slip sts, sc in Back Loop Only of each sc across.

Row 3: Ch 1, turn; sc in Back Loops Only of each sc across; slip st in both loops of next 2 sc on Foundation Rnd.

Rows 4-45: Repeat Rows 2 and 3, 21 times.

Joining Row: Ch 1, turn, with **wrong** sides of last row and beginning ch together, working in free loops of beginning ch and in Back Loops Only of sc on last row, slip st in each st across; finish off.

True Story

I am surprised at how often I find myself slipping these on. In my car, I keep a pair of them in my glove compartment for chilly mornings. More often than not, putting them on is the first thing I do when I get in my car!

I love that they are fingerless mitts so I can still buckle my seatbelt and turn on the ignition with them on without having to worry about accidentally clipping a piece of the fabric. You will find that you love them too.

Thistle Mitts

BASIC

I love learning new stitches and turning them into something that I can wear. While doing a swatch for the thistle stitch I fell in love with it and knew I had to make a pair of fingerless mitts. Thus, the thistle fingerless mitts were born. This fun stitch pattern makes for a dense fabric with a lot of texture. Coupled with the Hygge Charm yarn and its hint of sparkle, these mitts are must-haves!

Shopping List

Yarn (Bulky Weight)

BULKY 5

[5 ounces, 132 yards (141 grams, 121 meters) per skein]:

☐ 1 skein

Crochet Hook

☐ Size I (5.5 mm) **or** size needed for gauge

Finished Size:

9¼" long x 9" hand circumference (23.5 cm x 23 cm)

GAUGE INFORMATION

In pattern,
(sc3tog, ch 1) 5 times = 3" (7.5 cm);
11 rows = 4" (10 cm)

Gauge Swatch: 3" wide x 4" high (7.5 cm x 10 cm)

Ch 12.

Work same as Body for 11 rows: 5 sc3tog, 4 ch-1 sps, and 2 sc.

Finish off.

STITCH GUIDE

SINGLE CROCHET 3 TOGETHER
(abbreviated sc3tog)
(uses **next** 2 sts or sps)

Insert hook in same st or sp as last st made, YO and pull up a loop, (insert hook in **next** st or sp, YO and pull up loop) twice, YO and draw through all 4 loops on hook.

MITT (Make 2)

Body

Ch 30.

Matchy Matchy:

Make a cowl or scarf to match the mitts!

Row 1 (Wrong side)**:** Sc in second ch from hook and in each ch across: 29 sc.

Note: Loop a short piece of yarn around the **back** of any stitch on Row 1 to mark **right** side.

Row 2: Ch 1, turn; sc in first sc, sc3tog, (ch 1, sc3tog) across, sc in same st as last st: 14 sc3tog, 13 ch-1 sps, and 2 sc.

Repeat Row 2 until piece measures approximately 9" (23 cm) from beginning ch; do **not** finish off.

Joining Row: Ch 1, turn; fold piece in half with **right** side together, matching beginning ch to last row. Working through **both** loops on **both** pieces, slip st in first 17 sts, working in **both** loops of sts on front piece only, slip st in next 5 sts **(thumb opening)**, working through **both** loops on **both** pieces, slip st in last 7 sts; do **not** finish off.

Trim

Rnd 1: Ch 1, turn Mitt right side out, working in ends of rows, work 25 sc evenly spaced around; do **not** join, place marker to indicate beginning of round ***(see Markers, page 58)***.

Rnd 2: Sc in each sc around; slip st in next sc, finish off.

Tip from Marly

When it is time to seam up the mitts, try them on as you go to make sure the thumb hole is large enough for your hand. If you need it a little larger simply leave more stitches unworked for the thumb opening, and vice versa if you need it smaller.

Wavy Mitts

BASIC

So much fun to make, these mitts are made in two pieces then seamed together to get a nice cuff that can be rolled up or left flat. I love doing simple stitches that have a lot of texture. These mitts hit the mark for me. Go ahead and give them a try, you are going to fall in love!

Shopping List

Yarn (Medium Weight)

MEDIUM 4

[3.5 ounces, 198 yards (100 grams, 181 meters) per skein]:

☐ Pink - 1 skein

☐ Grey - 1 skein

Crochet Hook

☐ Size G (4 mm) **or** size needed for gauge

Finished Size:
10½" long x 8" circumference (26.5 cm x 20.5 cm)

GAUGE INFORMATION

In Cuff pattern, 16 sc = 4" (10 cm)
In Body pattern, 20 sts = 4" (10 cm)
Gauge Swatch: 4" (10 cm) square
Ch 21.
Work same as Body for 9 rows: 20 sts.
Finish off.

MITT (Make 2)

Body

With Pink, ch 29.

Work slip sts very loosely so it is easy to work into them on subsequent rows.

Row 1 (Right side)**:** Slip st in second ch from hook and in next 3 chs, ★ hdc in next 4 chs, slip st in next 4 chs; repeat from ★ across: 28 sts.

Note: Loop a short piece of yarn around any stitch to mark Row 1 as **right** side.

Row 2: Ch 1, turn; working in Back Loops Only, slip st in first 4 slip sts, ★ hdc in next 4 hdc, slip st in next 4 slip sts; repeat from ★ across.

Row 3: Ch 2 **(counts as first hdc, now and throughout)**, turn; working in Back Loops Only, hdc in next 3 slip sts, ★ slip st in next 4 hdc, hdc in next 4 slip sts; repeat from ★ across.

Row 4: Ch 2, turn; working in Back Loops Only, hdc in next 3 hdc, ★ slip st in next 4 slip sts, hdc in next 4 hdc; repeat from ★ across.

Row 5: Ch 1, turn; working in Back Loops Only, slip st in first 4 hdc, ★ hdc in next 4 slip sts, slip st in next 4 hdc; repeat from ★ across.

Row 6: Ch 1, turn; working in Back Loops Only, slip st in first 4 slip sts, ★ hdc in next 4 hdc, slip st in next 4 slip sts; repeat from ★ across.

Repeat Rows 3-6 for pattern until Body measures approximately 8" (20.5 cm) from beginning ch, ending by working a **right** side row.

Trim: Ch 1, do **not** turn; working in ends of rows, work 40 sc evenly spaced across; finish off leaving a long end for sewing.

Joining row: With **wrong** sides of last row and beginning ch together, working in free loops of beginning ch and in both loops of sc on last row, whipstitch seam for 2" (5 cm) ***(Fig. 7, page 59)***, leaving a 1¾" (4.5 cm) thumb opening, whipstitch remaining seam together.

Cuff

With Grey, ch 21.

Row 1: Sc in second ch from hook and in each ch across: 20 sc.

Row 2: Ch 1, turn; sc in Back Loop Only of each sc across.

Repeat Row 2 until Cuff measures approximately 8" (20.5 cm); do **not** finish off.

Trim: Ch 1, do **not** turn; working in ends of rows, work 40 sc evenly spaced across.

Joining Row: With **wrong** sides of last row and beginning ch together, working in free loops of beginning ch and in both loops of sc on last row, slip st in each sc across; finish off.

With **right** sides of Body and Cuff together, matching sc on Trim and seams and working through **both** loops of **both** sc, join Grey with slip st in first sc; slip st in each sc around; join with slip st to first slip st, finish off.

Bright Idea!

Add some buttons on the outside of the cuffs for style rather than function. They would really jazz up an already cute pair of mitts.

Change it up!

Make the granny squares with scrap yarn! Like the granny afghans of old, use the scrap yarn balled up in your basket to make these fun mitts.

Granny Warmers

BASIC

What would any book be without a granny square? These hand warmers are just the right size. Made with a long color changing yarn, each hand warmer is subtly different but still match. If you have mastered the granny square, then you will have no problem with this project.

Shopping List

Yarn (Medium Weight)

[5.29 ounces, 296 yards (150 grams, 271 meters) per skein]:

☐ 1 skein

Crochet Hook

☐ Size I (5.5 mm)
or size needed for gauge

Finished Size:
6½" long x 8" hand circumference (16.5 cm x 20.5 cm)

GAUGE INFORMATION

Gauge Swatch: 4" (10 cm) square
Work same as Granny Square: 18 dc.
Finish off.

STITCH GUIDE

BACK POST DOUBLE CROCHET
(abbreviated BPdc)
YO, insert hook in from **back** to **front** around post of st indicated ***(Fig. A)***, YO and pull up a loop (3 loops on hook), (YO and draw through 2 loops on hook) twice

FRONT POST DOUBLE CROCHET
(abbreviated FPdc)
YO, insert hook from **front** to **back** around post of st indicated ***(Fig. A)***, YO and pull up a loop (3 loops on hook), (YO and draw through 2 loops on hook) twice.

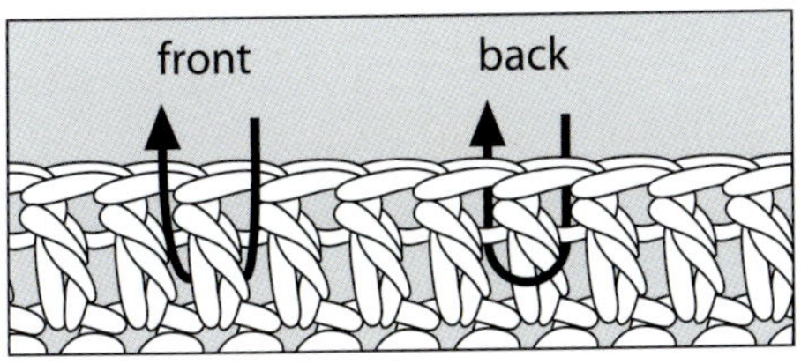

Fig. A

MITT **(Make 2)**

Motif (Make 2)

Rnd 1 (Right side)**:** Ch 4, 2 dc in fourth ch from hook **(3 skipped chs count as first dc)**, (ch 1, 3 dc in same ch) 3 times, sc in first dc to form last ch-1 sp: 12 dc and 4 ch-1 sps.

Rnd 2: Ch 3 **(counts as first dc, now and throughout)**, 2 dc in last ch-1 sp made, ch 1, ★ (3 dc, ch 1, 3 dc) in next ch-1 sp, ch 1; repeat from ★ 2 times **more**, 3 dc in same sp as first dc, sc in first dc to form last ch-1 sp: 24 dc and 8 ch-1 sps.

Rnd 3: Ch 3, 2 dc in last ch-1 sp made, ch 1, 3 dc in next ch-1 sp, ch 1, ★ (3 dc, ch 1, 3 dc) in next ch-1 sp, ch 1, 3 dc in next ch-1 sp, ch 1; repeat from ★ 2 times **more**, 3 dc in same sp as first dc, sc in first dc to form last ch-1 sp: 36 dc and 12 ch-1 sps.

Rnd 4: Ch 1, sc in last ch-1 sp made and in each dc and each ch-1 sp around; join with slip st to Back Loop Only of first sc ***(Fig. 2, page 59)***, do **not** finish off: 48 sc.

First Side Joining

With **wrong** sides together and working through **inside** loops only, slip st in same sc and in next 2 sc, working in Back Loop Only of sc on front piece only, slip in next 5 sc, working through **inside** loops only, slip st in next 5 sc; finish off.

Second Side Joining

With **wrong** sides together, working through **inside** loops only, join yarn with slip st in next corner sc from First Side Joining; slip st in next 12 sc; do **not** finish off.

Top Trim

Rnd 1: Working in Back Loops Only, ch 2 **(counts as first hdc, now and throughout)**, hdc in next 11 sc, hdc in same st as joining, skip next joining, hdc in same st as joining on next Motif and in next 11 sc, hdc in same st as next joining; join with slip st to first hdc: 26 hdc.

Rnds 2 and 3: Ch 2, hdc in horizontal bar of next hdc and each hdc around ***(Fig. 4, page 59)***; join with slip st to first hdc.

Finish off.

Cuff

Rnd 1: With **right** side facing, join yarn with dc in same st as First Side Joining *(see Joining With Dc, page 58)*; dc in next 11 sc and in same st as joining, skip joining, dc in same st as joining on next Motif and in next 11 sc, dc in same st as joining; join with slip st to first dc: 26 dc.

Rnds 2-5: Slip st from **back** to **front** around same st, ch 2 (**counts as first BPdc**), work FPdc around next st ★ work BPdc around next st, work FPdc around next st; repeat from ★ around; join with slip st to first st.

Finish off.

General Instructions

ABBREVIATIONS

BPdc	Back Post double crochet(s)
ch(s)	chain(s)
cm	centimeters
dc	double crochet(s)
dc2tog	double crochet 2 together
FPdc	Front Post double crochet(s)
hdc	half double crochet(s)
hdc2tog	half double crochet 2 together
mm	millimeters
sc	single crochet(s)
sc3tog	single crochet 3 together
sp(s)	space(s)
st(s)	stitch(es)
YO	yarn over

CROCHET TERMINOLOGY		
UNITED STATES		INTERNATIONAL
slip stitch (slip st)	=	single crochet (sc)
single crochet (sc)	=	double crochet (dc)
half double crochet (hdc)	=	half treble crochet (htr)
double crochet (dc)	=	treble crochet (tr)
treble crochet (tr)	=	double treble crochet (dtr)
double treble crochet (dtr)	=	triple treble crochet (ttr)
triple treble crochet (tr tr)	=	quadruple treble crochet (qtr)
skip	=	miss

SYMBOLS & TERMS

★ — work instructions following ★ as many **more** times as indicated in addition to the first time.

( ) or **[ ]** — work the enclosed instructions **as many** times as specified by the number immediately following **or** work all enclosed instructions in stitch or space indicated **or** contains explanatory remarks.

colon — the number(s) given after a colon at the end of a row or round denote(s) the number of stitches or spaces you should have on that row or round.

Yarn Weight Symbol & Names	LACE 0	SUPER FINE 1	FINE 2	LIGHT 3	MEDIUM 4	BULKY 5	SUPER BULKY 6	JUMBO 7
Type of Yarns in Category	Fingering, size 10 crochet thread	Sock, Fingering, Baby	Sport, Baby	DK, Light Worsted	Worsted, Afghan, Aran	Chunky, Craft, Rug	Super Bulky, Roving	Jumbo, Roving
Crochet Gauge* Ranges in Single Crochet to 4" (10 cm)	32-42 sts**	21-32 sts	16-20 sts	12-17 sts	11-14 sts	8-11 sts	6-9 sts	5 sts and fewer
Advised Hook Size Range	Steel*** 6 to 8, Regular hook B-1	B-1 to E-4	E-4 to 7	7 to I-9	I-9 to K-10½	K-10½ to M/N-13	M/N-13 to Q	Q and larger

*GUIDELINES ONLY: The chart above reflects the most commonly used gauges and hook sizes for specific yarn categories.

** Lace weight yarns are usually crocheted with larger hooks to create lacy openwork patterns. Accordingly, a gauge range is difficult to determine. Always follow the gauge stated in your pattern.

*** Steel crochet hooks are sized differently from regular hooks -the higher the number, the smaller the hook, which is the reverse of regular hook sizing.

■□□□ **BASIC**	Projects using basic stitches. May include basic increases and decreases.
■■□□ **EASY**	Projects may include simple stitch patterns, color work, and/or shaping.
■■■□ **INTERMEDIATE**	Projects may include involved stitch patterns, color work, and/or shaping.
■■■■ **COMPLEX**	Projects may include complex stitch patterns, color work, and/or shaping using a variety of techniques and stitches simultaneously.

CROCHET HOOKS																	
U.S.	B-1	C-2	D-3	E-4	F-5	G-6	7	H-8	I-9	J-10	K-10½	L-11	M/N-13	N/P-15	P/Q	Q	S
Metric - mm	2.25	2.75	3.25	3.5	3.75	4	4.5	5	5.5	6	6.5	8	9	10	15	16	19

GAUGE

Exact gauge is essential for proper size. Before beginning your project, make the sample swatch given in the individual instructions in the yarn and hook specified. After completing the swatch, measure it, counting your stitches and rows carefully. If your swatch is larger or smaller than specified, **make another, changing the hook size to get the correct gauge**. Keep trying until you find the size that will give you the specified gauge.

JOINING WITH SC

When instructed to join with sc, begin with a slip knot on hook. Insert hook in stitch or space indicated, YO and pull up a loop, YO and draw through both loops on hook.

JOINING WITH HDC

When instructed to join with a hdc, begin with a slip knot on the hook. YO, holding loop on hook, insert hook in stitch or space indicated, YO and pull up a loop (3 loops on hook), YO and draw through 3 loops on hook.

JOINING WITH DC

When instructed to join with a dc, begin with a slip knot on the hook. YO, holding loop on hook, insert hook in stitch or space indicated, YO and pull up a loop (3 loops on hook), (YO and draw through 2 loops on hook) twice.

MARKERS

Markers are used to help distinguish the beginning of each round being worked. Place a 2" (5 cm) scrap piece of yarn before the first stitch of each round, moving the marker after each round is complete.

ADJUSTABLE LOOP

Wind the yarn around two fingers to form a ring ***(Fig. 1a)***, slide the yarn off your fingers and grasp the strands at the top of the ring ***(Fig. 1b)***. Insert the hook from **front** to **back** into the ring, pull up a loop, YO and draw through the loop on hook to lock the ring ***(Fig. 1c)***.

Working around **both** strands, work stitches in the ring as specified, then pull the yarn end to close ***(Fig. 1d)***.

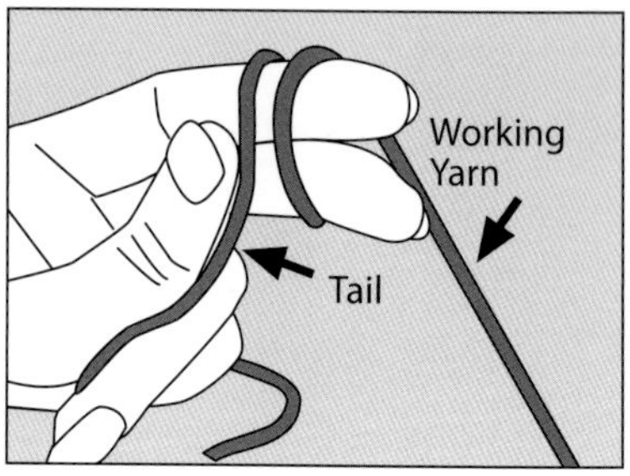

Fig. 1a

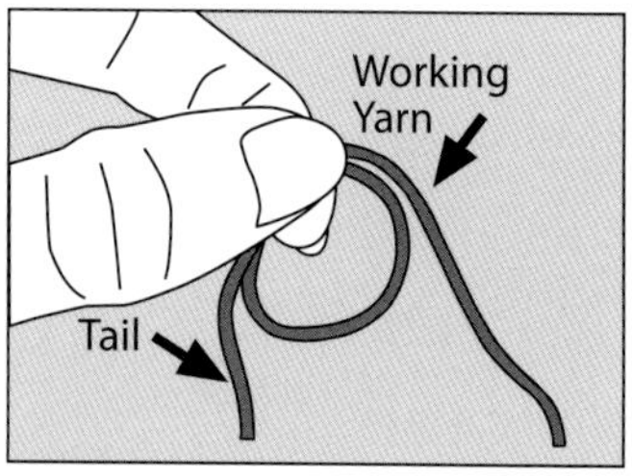

Fig. 1b

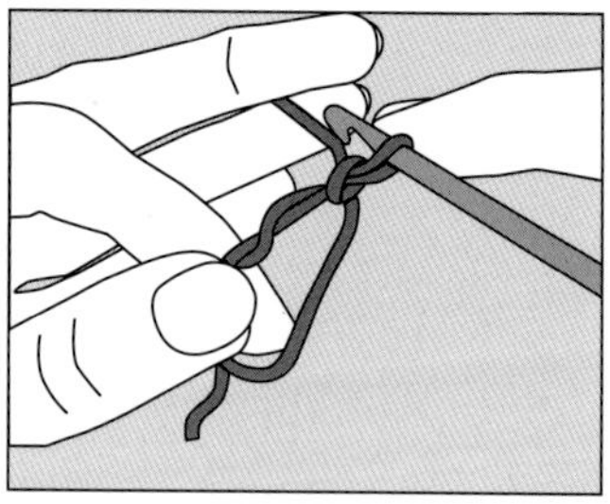

Fig. 1c

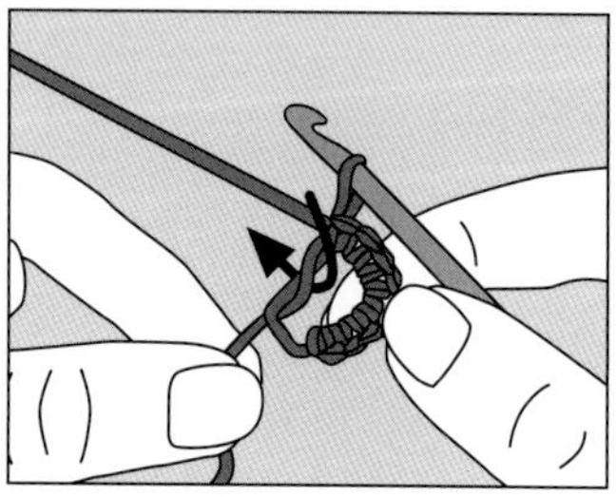

Fig. 1d

BACK LOOP ONLY

Work only in loop(s) indicated by arrow ***(Fig. 2)***.

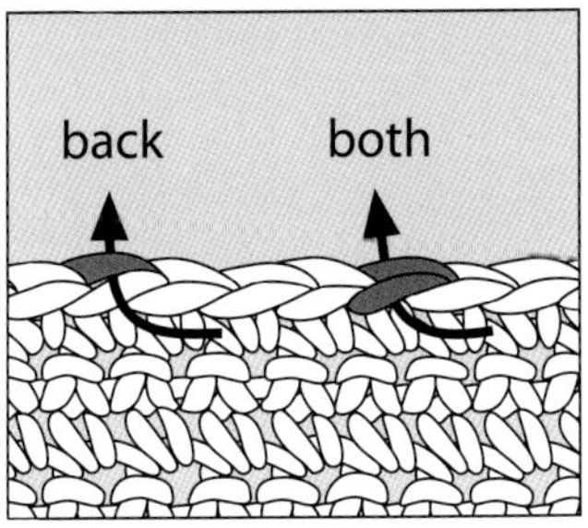

Fig. 2

FREE LOOPS OF A CHAIN

When instructed to work in free loops of a chain, work in loop indicated by arrow ***(Fig. 3)***.

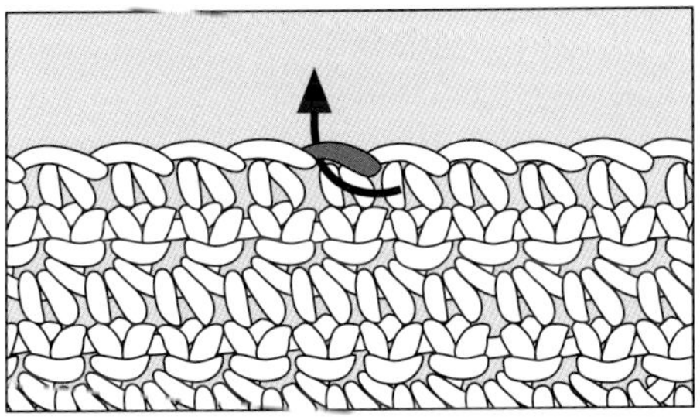

Fig. 3

WORKING IN HORIZONTAL BAR

YO, insert hook in horizontal bar of hdc indicated, YO and pull up a loop ***(Fig. 4)***.

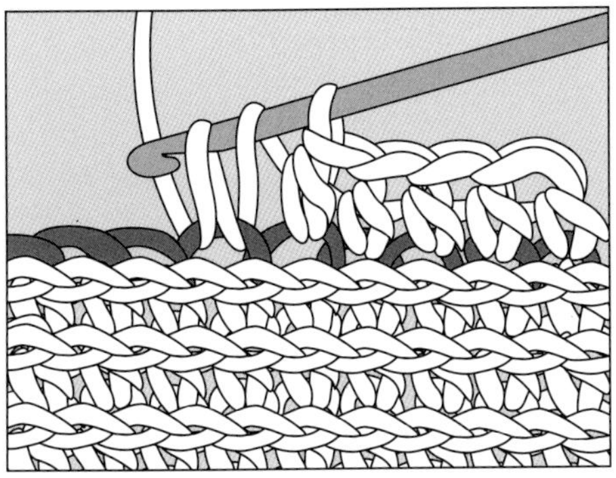

Fig. 4

WEAVE THRU STITCHES

Weave yarn end through the stitches ***(Fig. 5)*** and gather to close.

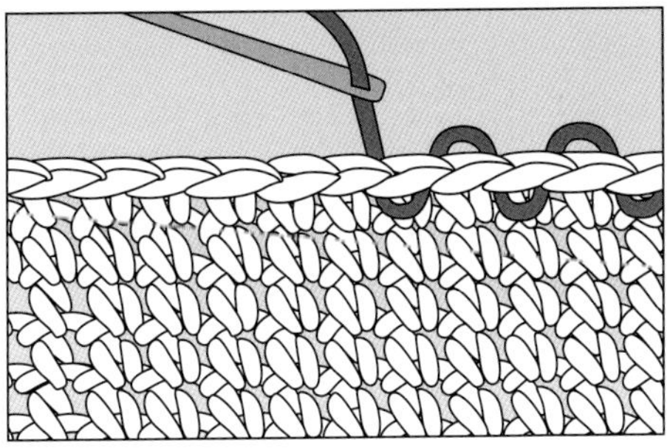

Fig. 5

CHANGING COLORS

Work the last stitch to within one step of completion, hook new yarn ***(Fig. 6)*** and draw through all loops on hook.

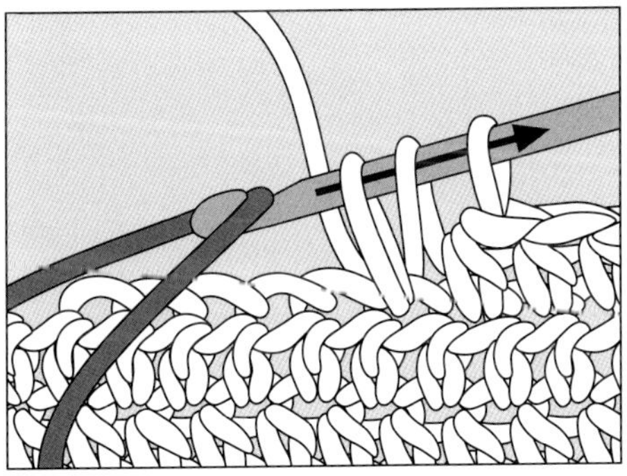

Fig. 6

WHIPSTITCH

With **right** side together, sew through stitches on both sides once to secure the beginning of the seam, leaving an ample yarn end to weave in later. Insert the needle from **back** to **front** through **both** loops on **both** sides ***(Fig. 7)***. Bring the needle around and insert it from **back** to **front** through next loops of both sides. Continue in this manner across, keeping the sewing yarn fairly loose.

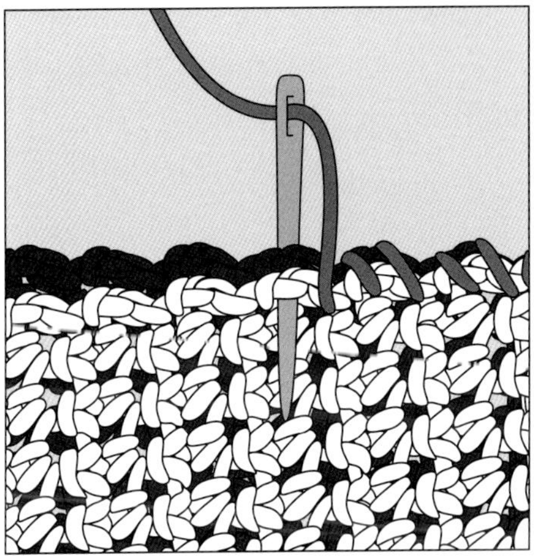

Fig. 7

Basic Crochet Stitches

CHAIN

To work a chain stitch, begin with a slip knot on the hook. Bring the yarn **over** hook from back to front, catching the yarn with the hook and turning the hook slightly toward you to keep the yarn from slipping off. Draw the yarn through the slip knot ***(Fig. 8)*** **(first chain st made, *abbreviated ch*)**.

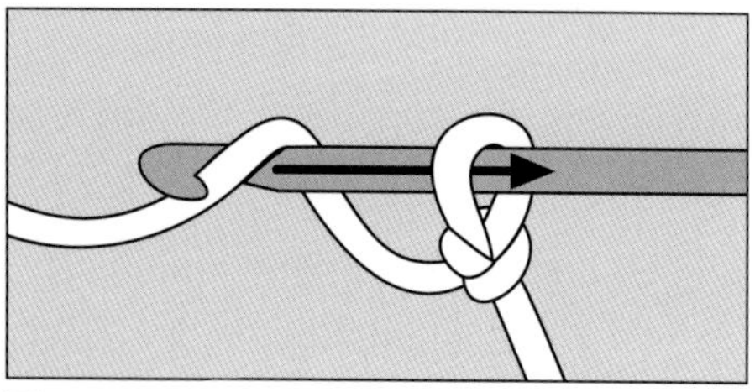

Fig. 8

WORKING INTO THE CHAIN

Method 1: Insert hook into back ridge of each chain ***(Fig. 9a)***.

Method 2: Insert hook under top two strands of each chain ***(Fig. 9b)***.

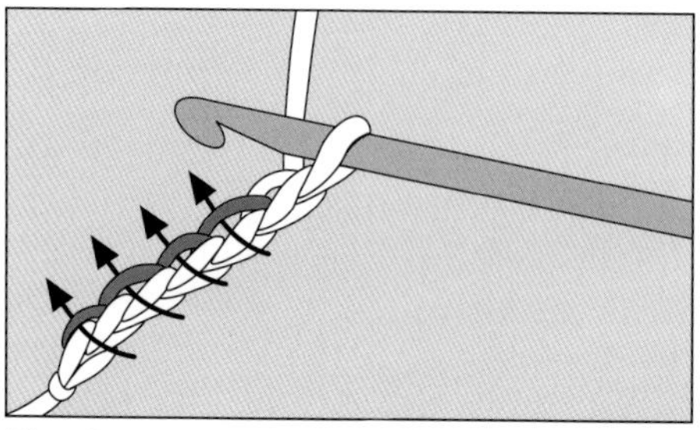

Fig. 9a

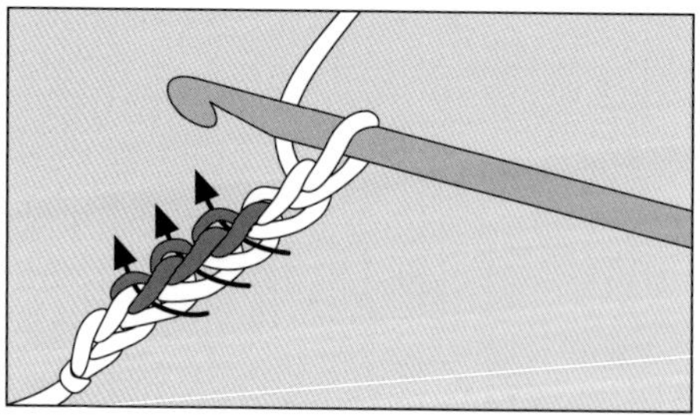

Fig. 9b

SLIP STITCH

To work a slip stitch, insert hook in stitch indicated, YO and draw through st and through loop on hook ***(Fig. 10)*** **(slip stitch made, *abbreviated slip st*)**.

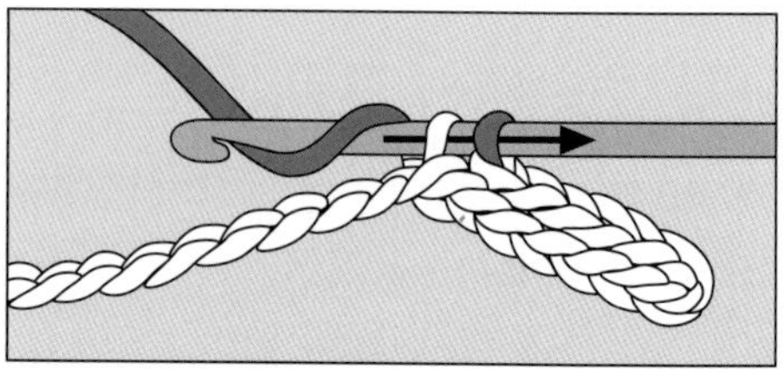

Fig. 10

SINGLE CROCHET

Insert hook in stitch indicated, YO and pull up a loop, YO and draw through both loops on hook ***(Fig. 11)*** **(single crochet made, *abbreviated sc*)**.

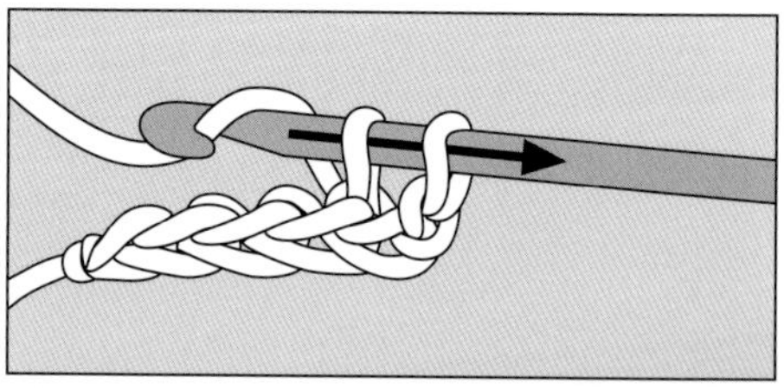

Fig. 11

HALF DOUBLE CROCHET

YO, insert hook in stitch indicated, YO and pull up a loop, YO and draw through all 3 loops on hook *(Fig. 12)* **(half double crochet made, *abbreviated hdc*)**.

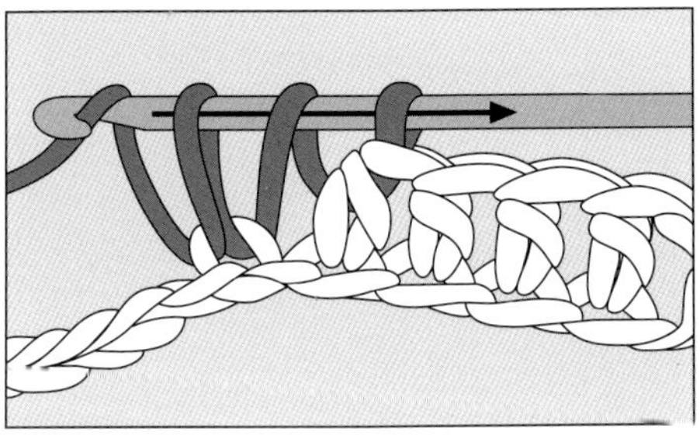

Fig. 12

DOUBLE CROCHET

YO, insert hook in stitch indicated, YO and pull up a loop (3 loops on hook), YO and draw through 2 loops on hook *(Fig. 13a)*, YO and draw through remaining 2 loops on hook *(Fig. 13b)* **(double crochet made, *abbreviated dc*)**.

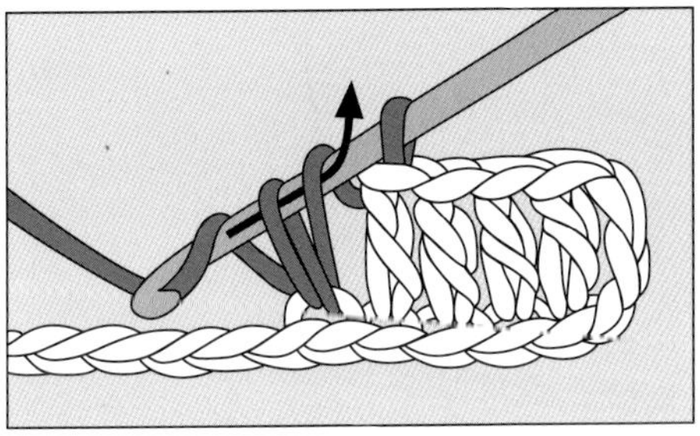

Fig. 13a

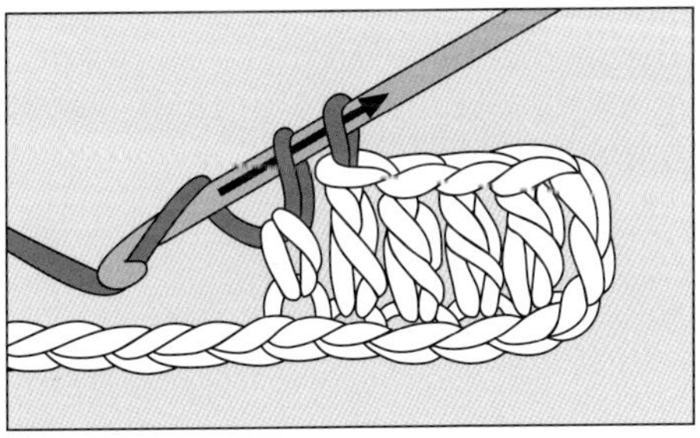

Fig. 13b

TREBLE CROCHET

YO twice, insert hook in stitch Indicated, YO and pull up a loop (4 loops on hook), (YO and draw through 2 loops on hook) 3 times *(Figs. 14a & b)* **(treble crochet made, *abbreviated tr*)**.

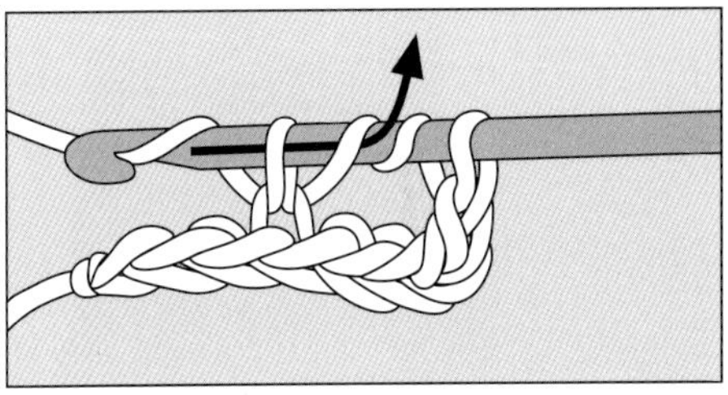

Fig. 14a

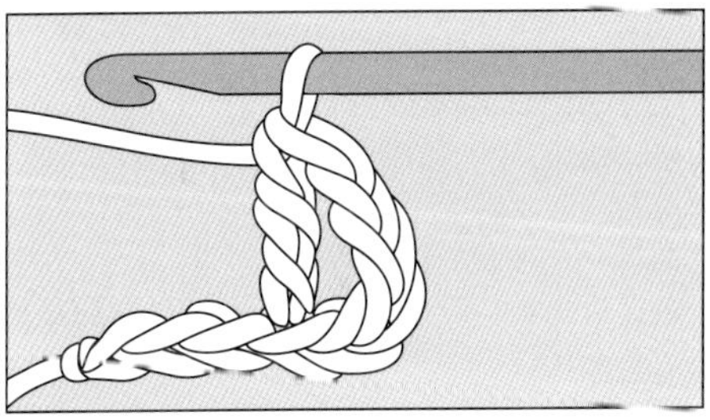

Fig. 14b

Yarn Information

The Hand Warmers in this book were made using various weights of yarn. Any brand of the specified yarn weight may be used. It is best to refer to the yardage/meters when determining how many balls or skeins to purchase. Remember, to arrive at the finished size, it is the GAUGE/TENSION that is important, not the brand of yarn.

For your convenience, the specific yarns used to create our photography models are listed. Because yarn manufacturers make frequent changes in their product lines, you may sometimes find it necessary to use a substitute yarn or to search for the discontinued product at alternate suppliers (locally or online).

BASIC WRISTERS
Red Heart® Chic Sheep by Marly Bird™
#5390 Lipstick

BASIC MITTENS
Red Heart® Sweet Home™
#411 Steel

HYGGE MUFF
Red Heart® Hygge™
Grey - #8339 Cloud
Red Heart® Sweet Home™
Dark Grey - #411 Steel

RUNNER'S MITTS
Red Heart® Reflective™
Purple - #8532 Purple
Grey - #8429 Grey

SCRAPPY WARMERS
Red Heart® Chic Sheep by Marly Bird™
Brown - #5365 Leather
Blue - #5693 Poolside
Green - #5620 Green Tea
Pink - #5622 Dragon Fruit

RAINBOW MITTENS
Red Heart® Colorscape™
#9356 Acapulco

STRIPED WARMERS
Red Heart® With Love™
Ecru - #1306 Stone
Brown - #1970 Taupe
Rust - #1936 Terracotta
Grey - #1441 Light Grey

THISTLE MITTS
Red Heart® Hygge Charm™
#6579 Evening Star

WAVY MITTS
Red Heart® Amore™
Pink - #6724 Peaceful
Grey - #6341 Earl Grey

GRANNY WARMERS
Red Heart® Roll With It Tweed™
#9526 Lilac Breeze

We have made every effort to ensure that these instructions are accurate and complete. We cannot, however, be responsible for human error, typographical mistakes, or variations in individual work.

Production Team: Instructional/Technical Editor - Lois J. Long; Senior Graphic Artist - Lora Puls; Graphic Artist - Lori S. Malkin; Photo Stylist - Lori Wenger; and Photographer - Jason Masters.

Library of Congress Control Number: 2019940082

Made in U.S.A.